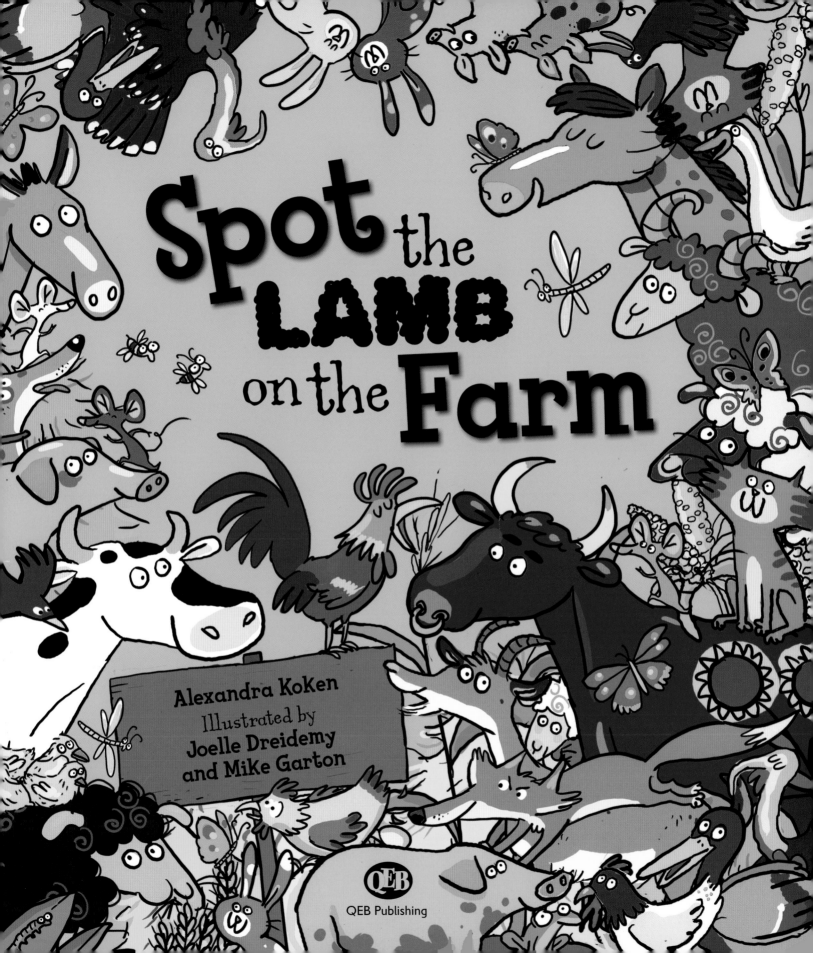

Spot the LAMB on the Farm

Alexandra Koken

Illustrated by
Joelle Dreidemy
and Mike Garton

QEB Publishing

Sheep

Farm Vehicles

Wheat

Cows

Stables

This lamb is hiding
in every scene.
Can you find her?

Can you spot these things?

cat flower frog teakettle shoe

Cock-a-doodle-doo!

Donkeys love to make friends with other animals.

Can you spot these things?

umbrella   book   trampoline   green apple   towel

Mud helps pigs cool down.

Can you spot these things? donkey underwear duck spoon bell

Tractors are slow, but very powerful.

When they were first discovered, carrots were purple!

Can you spot these things?

squirrel   worm   button

onion   pumpkin

Can you spot these things?

cow   toothbrush   cupcake   spider's web   chicken

There are hundreds of types, or breeds, of horses.

Bread, pasta, and cereals are often made from wheat.

Can you spot these things? watch   scales   tire   comb   sock

A sheep's fleecy coat can be used to make yarn.

More to Spot

Go back and find these scenes in the book!

Did you find me?

Did You Know?

A chicken can lay about 300 eggs per year. That's almost one a day!

Sheep eat for about seven hours every day.

After cows have swallowed their food, it comes back into their mouths so they can chew it again.

Pigs are very clever and friendly. They make great pets!

A single ant can lift 20 times its body weight. That's like you lifting a tiger!

More Farm Fun!

Farm Sounds

The animals in this book make very different sounds, from "Moo" to "Meow" and "Cock-a-doodle-doo." When you see an animal in the book, make the sound!

Vegetable Patch

Growing vegetables is fun! You can grow small plants such as bean sprouts or herbs at home, or bigger plants such as tomatoes and carrots in a garden. You'll need seeds, soil, sunshine, and water. Remember to ask an adult for permission and help!

Hide-and-Seek

Choose a stuffed animal that you can hide around your home for a friend or family member to spot, just like the lamb in the book! You could hide other objects and make a list of things to find.

Life Cycles

Use books or the Internet to learn about the life cycle of some of the animals you've seen in this book. For example, an egg is laid by an adult chicken, and then hatches into a chick. The chick grows into an adult, which lays more eggs itself.

Designer: Krina Patel
Managing Editor: Victoria Garrard
Design Manager: Anna Lubecka

Copyright © QEB Publishing, Inc. 2013

First published in the United States by
QEB Publishing, Inc.
3 Wrigley, Suite A
Irvine, CA 92618

www.qed-publishing.co.uk

A CIP record for this book is available from the Library of Congress.

ISBN 978 1 60992 529 1

Printed in China